Handy Pennsylvania Genealogy Handbook

I0435613

Gary L. Morris

Dedication

To everyone with a love of family and who wants to find
more of them.

Acknowledgments

Every genealogy researcher and volunteer who has taken the time to find and share the valuable resources we all need to find our family members.

Table of Contents

Notes

Notes

Genealogical Research in Pennsylvania

As one of the original thirteen colonies, there are many genealogical records and resources available for tracing your family history in Pennsylvania. Because there are so many records held at many different locations, tracking down the records for your ancestor can be an ominous task. Don't worry though, we know just where they are, and we'll show you which records you'll need, while helping you to understand:

1. What they are
2. Where to find them
3. How to use them

These records can be found both online and off, so we'll introduce you to online websites, indexes and databases, as well as brick-and-mortar repositories and other institutions that will help with your research in Pennsylvania. So that you will have a more comprehensive understanding of these records, we have provided a brief history of the "Keystone State" to illustrate what type of records may have been generated during specific time periods. That information will assist you in pinpointing times and locations on which to focus the search for your Pennsylvania ancestors and their records.

A Brief History of Pennsylvania

Cornelis Jacobssen was most likely the first European to reach Pennsylvania when he explored the area for Dutch Merchants in 1614. The Swedes began establishing farms in the region in 1638, and they lived in peace with the local Indians with whom they traded furs. The Dutch took control of the region when they defeated New Sweden in 1655, but surrendered the land to the British in 1664. The British conquest was partly financed by the father of William Penn for whom the state is named, and to whom the land was given.

As owner of Pennsylvania, William Penn had the power to legislate laws, levy taxes, declare war, print money, appoint officials, sell land, and administer judgment. Penn drafted Pennsylvania's first charter, the Frame of Government in 1682, although those policies were enforced for just one year. In the same year he approved the location and layout for Philadelphia, and established a Second Frame of Government in 1683. The same year saw the settlement of Germantown begin.

Arriving in the colony in October 1682, Penn approved the location and layout of Philadelphia, met with the Leni-Lenape to acquire land and exchange vows of peace, called for elections to select an assembly, and proposed a Great Law that ranged from prescribing weights and measures to guaranteeing fundamental liberties.

With the evolvement of government came an attraction to settlers, and in addition to the German settlers at Germantown, many English, Welsh, and Scots-Irish also flocked to the Philadelphia area. By 1776, those nationalities, in addition to French Huguenots and Black Slaves made up the majority of Pennsylvania's non-native population.

After the British victory in the French and Indian War, Pennsylvania moved rapidly toward independence. Western Pennsylvanians were outraged at the Proclamation of 1763, which prevented settlement west of the Alleghenies, and all Philadelphians were further incensed at the implementation of the Stamp Act of 1765, the Townshend Acts of 1767, and the Tea Act in1773. In spite of this, only three Pennsylvania delegates to the Second Continental Congress voted for independence in July 1776. Nevertheless, the Declaration of Independence was proclaimed from Pennsylvania's State House, Independence Hall, on 4 July 1776.

As the headquarters of the new American Congress, Philadelphia was an important target for the British during the War of Independence. The British occupied the city after defeating the Americans at the Battle of Brandywine Creek in September, 1777, and moved the provisional capitol first to Lancaster and then to York. General George Washington set up his famous winter headquarters at Valley Forge after battles at Germantown and Whitemarsh, and remained there until June 1778. The British evacuated Philadelphia during the spring of 1778, fearing French naval power intervening on behalf of the Americans, and Congress reconvened there on 2 July. Philadelphia continues to serve as the US capital until 1783, and again from 1790 to 1800.

Philadelphia adopted its state constitution in 1776 following independence, and in 1780 Pennsylvania passed the first state law abolishing slavery. Pennsylvania became the second state to ratify the US Constitution seven years later, and joined the Union. Industrialization began to grow in the state, and Pittsburgh's first iron furnace was built in 1792. The 1840s saw both an influx of Irish immigrants and the rise of the Native American (Know-Nothing) Party, an anti-Catholic movement.

Pennsylvania rallied to the Union cause at the outbreak of civil war, supplying some 338,000 men to the Union forces. The state was the scene of the Battle of Gettysburg in July 1863, a major turning point in the war for the Union cause, as the Confederate forces had to retreat to Virginia. After the Civil War Pennsylvania became the nation's chief supplier of iron, coal, and steel, and for much of that period the main source of lumber and petroleum.

Important Dates in Philadelphia History

1681 – Area granted to William Penn

1682 – Penn drafts First Frame of Government

1683 – Settlement of Germantown begins

1717 – Scotts-Irish begin to emigrate from Ulster

1753 – French troops build Fort Duquesne

1754 – French and Indian War begins in Pennsylvania

1758 – British capture Fort Duquesne

1776 – Declaration of independence signed in Philadelphia

1777 – State Constitution adopted

1863 – Battle of Gettysburg

Famous Battles Fought in Pennsylvania

Philadelphia has been the scene of many Battles, fought in many wars. Many battles were fought during the **American Revolution**, and the **French and Indian War** began in Pennsylvania. The **Battle of Gettysburg** was the only major Civil War battle fought in the state.

These battle accounts that exist can be very effective in uncovering the military records of your ancestor. They can tell you what regiments fought in which battles, and often include the names and ranks of many officers and enlisted men.

American Revolution:
http://explorepahistory.com/story.php?storyId=1-9-11&chapter=4

French and Indian War :
http://explorepahistory.com/story.php?storyId=1-9-6&chapter=0

Battle of Gettysburg:
http://www.nps.gov/hps/abpp/battles/pa002.htm

Common Philadelphia Genealogical Issues and Resources to Overcome Them

Boundary Changes: Boundary changes are a common obstacle when researching Philadelphia ancestors. You could be searching for an ancestor's record in one county when in fact it is stored in a different one due to historical county boundary changes.

The **Atlas of Historical County Boundaries** can help you to overcome that problem. It provides a chronological listing of every boundary change that has occurred in the history of Philadelphia.

Atlas of Historical County Boundaries :
http://publications.newberry.org/ahcbp/documents/PA_Consolidated_Chronology.htm#Consolidated_Chronology

Name Changes: Surname changes, variations, and misspellings can complicate genealogical research. It is important to check all spelling variations. Soundex, a program that indexes names by sound, is a useful first step, but you can't rely on it completely as some name variations result in different Soundex codes. The surnames could be different, but the first name may be different too. You can also find records filed under initials, middle names, and nicknames as well, so you will need to **get creative with surname variations** and spellings in order to cover all the possibilities. For help with surname variations read our instructional article on **How to Use Soundex**.

get creative with surname variations :
http://obituarieshelp.org/blog/?p=634

How to Use Soundex : http://obituarieshelp.org/blog/?p=505

Philadelphia Genealogical Organizations and Archives

Genealogical resources include not only records, but the organizations that house them, or can direct you to them. These institutions include: *Archives, Libraries, Genealogical Societies, Family History Centers, Universities, Churches, and Museums.*

Following are links to their websites, their physical addresses, and a summary of the records you can find there.

Archives and Libraries

Pennsylvania State Archives – vital records, census records, land records, military records, county and municipal records, naturalization records, ship's passenger lists, railroad records, manuscripts, personal papers, and more

Mailing Address:

350 North Street
Harrisburg, PA 17108-1026
Phone: (717) 783-3281
E-mail: ra-statearchives@state.pa.us

Pennsylvania State Archives link to:
http://www.portal.state.pa.us/portal/server.pt?open=512&
mode=2&objID=2887

Pennsylvania State Library - wide variety of indexes, genealogies, state and county histories, atlases, land warranty maps, ship lists, and compilations of church and cemetery records, as well as the Pennsylvania Federal Census records on microfilm

607 South Drive
Harrisburg, Pennsylvania
Phone: (717) 783-5950

Pennsylvania State Library link to:
http://www.portal.state.pa.us/portal/server.pt/community /genealogy___local_history/8730/home

National Archives-Mid-Atlantic Region - Census Records, Ship's Passenger Lists, Naturalization Records, Military Service Records

900 Market Street
Philadelphia, PA 19107-4292
Phone: (215) 606-0100
Fax: (215) 606-0116

National Archives-Mid-Atlantic Region:
http://www.archives.gov/philadelphia/

Pennsylvania Genealogical and Historical Societies

Genealogical and historical societies have access to extensive catalogues of genealogical data. They are also able to offer expert guidance for genealogical researchers. Many members are professional genealogists who are most willing to share their expertise in finding ancestors.

Historical Society of Pennsylvania - Family Papers and Manuscript Collections, Wills, Probate Records, and Deeds, Tax Records, Church Records, Birth and Marriage Records, Death and Burial Records, Census Records, Passenger and Immigration Records, Newspapers and Periodicals

1300 Locust Street
Philadelphia, PA 19107
Tel: (215) 732-6200
Fax: (215) 732-2680

Historical Society of Pennsylvania:
http://hsp.org/collections/catalogs-research-tools/subject-guides/family-history-genealogy

Genealogical Society of Pennsylvania – naturalizations index, court records, newspaper index, county marriages index, church record indexes and transcriptions, burial and cemetery records and transcriptions, surname index and family histories

2207 Chestnut Street
Philadelphia, PA 19103-3010
Tel: (215) 545-0391

Genealogical Society of Pennsylvania : http://genpa.org/

Additional Pennsylvania Resources

<u>Pennsylvania Mailing Lists</u>

Mailing lists are internet based facilities that use email to distribute a single message to all who subscribe to it. When information on a particular surname, new records, or any other important genealogy information related to the mailing list topic becomes available, the subscribers are alerted to it. Joining a mailing list is an excellent way to stay up to date on Pennsylvania genealogy research topics. Rootsweb have an extensive listing of **Pennsylvania Mailing Lists** on a variety of topics.

Pennsylvania Mailing Lists :
http://lists.rootsweb.ancestry.com/index/usa/PA/misc.html

<u>Pennsylvania Message Boards</u>

A message board is another internet based facility where people can post questions about a specific genealogy topic and have it answered by other genealogists. If you have questions about a surname, record type, or research topic, you can post your question and other researchers and genealogists will help you with the answer. Be sure to check back regularly, as the answers are not emailed to you. The message boards at the **Pennsylvania Genealogy Forum** are completely free to use.

Pennsylvania Genealogy Forum:
http://genforum.genealogy.com/pa/

Pennsylvania Newspapers and Periodicals

Many genealogy periodicals and historical newspapers contain
reprinted copies of family genealogies, transcripts of family Bible
records, information about local records and archives, census
indexes, church records, queries, land records, obituaries, court
records, cemetery records, and wills. The following sites have
historical Pennsylvania newspapers and periodicals that you can
search online or on-site.

Historical Society of Pennsylvania - indexes to Poulson's Daily
Advertiser (1796-1839); the Philadelphia Public Ledger (1836-1875);
the Pennsylvania Inquirer and Daily Courier Marriages and Deaths
Index (1834-1854); the Index to Obituaries from the Sunday
Dispatch (1868-1883); and Necrology from the Bulletin Almanac
(1923-1966), and many more historical Pennsylvania newspapers

1300 Locust Street
Philadelphia, PA 19107
Tel: (215) 732-6200
Fax: (215) 732-2680

Historical Society of Pennsylvania:
http://hsp.org/collections/catalogs-research-tools/subject-
guides/family-history-genealogy

Genealogical Society of Pennsylvania – variety of newspaper
indexes from historical publications

2207 Chestnut Street
Philadelphia, PA 19103-3010
Tel: (215) 545-0391

Genealogical Society of Pennsylvania : http://genpa.org/

GenealogyBank.com – free searchable database of Pennsylvania newspaper archives, 1719–1995

GenealogyBank.com link to:
http://www.genealogybank.com/gbnk/newspapers/explore/USA/Pennsylvania/

The Online Books Page – links to historical Pennsylvania books and periodicals available for viewing online

The Online Books Page link to:
http://onlinebooks.library.upenn.edu/webbin/book/browse?type=subject&type=subject&key=pennsylvania

Library of Congress Digital Newspaper Directory – free searchable database of historical U.S. newspapers dating from 1690-present

Library of Congress Digital Newspaper Directory link to:
http://chroniclingamerica.loc.gov/search/titles/

NewspaperArchive.com – largest online database of historical newspapers in the world.

NewspaperArchive.com link to:
http://newspaperarchive.com/

Historical Pennsylvania Maps and Gazetteers

Maps are an integral part of genealogical research. They help us to locate landmarks, towns, cities, parishes, states, provinces, waterways and roads and streets. They also help us to determine when and where boundary changes might have taken place, and give us a visualization of the area we're researching in.

For locating place names, a gazetteer is the best possible resource for any genealogist. Gazetteers are also sometimes called "place name dictionaries", and can help you to locate the area in which you need to conduct research. Below are links to the maps and gazetteers for research in Pennsylvania.

Peabody GNIS Service – Pennsylvania:
http://peabody.research.yale.edu/cgi-bin/Query.GNIS?ST=Pennsylvania&SU=1

Color Landform Atlas – Pennsylvania :
http://fermi.jhuapl.edu/states/pa_0.html

1985 U.S. Atlas: http://www.livgenmi.com/1895/PA/

Pennsylvania Hometown Locator :
http://pennsylvania.hometownlocator.com/

Pennsylvania City Directories

City directories are similar to telephone directories in that they list the residents of a particular area. The difference though is what is important to genealogists, and that is they pre-date telephone directories. You can find an ancestor's information such as their street address, place of employment, occupation, or the name of their spouse. A one-stop-shop for finding city directories in Pennsylvania is the **Pennsylvania Online Historical Directories** which contains a listing of every available online historical directory related to Pennsylvania.

Pennsylvania Online Historical Directories:
https://sites.google.com/site/onlinedirectorysite/Home/usa/pa

Pennsylvania State Library – huge collection of historical city directories from every county in the state

607 South Drive
Harrisburg, Pennsylvania
Phone: (717) 783-5950

Pennsylvania State Library:
http://www.portal.state.pa.us/portal/server.pt/community/gene
alogy___local_history/8730/home

Pennsylvania Genealogical Records

<u>Birth, Death, Marriage and Divorce Records</u> – Also known as vital records, birth, death, and marriage certificates are the most basic, yet most important records attached to your ancestor. The reason for their importance is that they not only place your ancestor in a specific place at a definite time, but potentially connect the individual to other relatives. Below is a list of repositories and websites where you can find Pennsylvania vital records.

Birth and death records began to be recorded at the state level in Pennsylvania in 1906 and can be found at:

Division of Vital Records
P.O. Box 1528
New Castle, Pennsylvania, 16103-1528
Tel: (724) 656-3100

Division of Vital Records:
http://www.portal.state.pa.us/portal/server.pt/community/birth _and_death_certificates/11596

Marriage and divorce records may be found in individual **Pennsylvania County Courthouses** in the county where the event occurred.

Pennsylvania County Courthouses:
http://www.portal.state.pa.us/portal/server.pt/community/abou t_the_archives/3177/county_courthouses/382915

Pennsylvania State Archives – Birth Certificates, 1906-1907, Death Certificates, 1906-1962, County Births and Deaths, 1893-1906, Governor's Accounts, 1742-1763 includes lists of marriages for the periods 1742-1752 and 1759-1762, General Motion and Divorce Docket, 1750-1837 with references to divorces for the period 1800-1805, Marriage Bonds for Philadelphia County, 1784-1786, Divorce Papers, 1786-1815, Record and Indexes of Births, Deaths, and Marriages, 1852-1854 Record of Marriages, 1885-1891

Mailing Address:

350 North Street
Harrisburg, PA 17108-1026
Phone: (717) 783-3281
E-mail: ra-statearchives@state.pa.us

Pennsylvania State Archives:
http://www.portal.state.pa.us/portal/server.pt/community/gene
alogy/3183/vital_statistics/387291

Historical Society of Pennsylvania - Early Pennsylvania Births, 1675-1875, Pennsylvania Vital Records from the Pennsylvania Genealogical Magazine and the Pennsylvania Magazine of History and Biography, Marriage Records Recorded by Various Philadelphia Mayors and Aldermen: 1800-1895, Philadelphia Marriage Records Index and Register, 1860-1916, Philadelphia Death Register, 1860-1903

1300 Locust Street
Philadelphia, PA 19107
Tel: (215) 732-6200
Fax: (215) 732-2680

Historical Society of Pennsylvania link to:
http://hsp.org/collections/catalogs-research-tools/subject-
guides/family-history-genealogy

Family Search has the following indexes which can be searched online for free:

- Pennsylvania, Births and Christenings, 1709-1950
- Pennsylvania, County Marriages, 1885-1950
- Pennsylvania, Marriages, 1709-1940
- Pennsylvania, Philadelphia City Births, 1860-1906
- Pennsylvania, Philadelphia City Death Certificates, 1803-1915
- Pennsylvania, Philadelphia Marriage Indexes, 1885-1951
- Pennsylvania, Pittsburgh City Deaths, 1870-1905

Pennsylvania, Births and Christenings, 1709-1950:
https://familysearch.org/search/collection/1681005

Pennsylvania, County Marriages, 1885-1950:
https://familysearch.org/search/collection/1589502

Pennsylvania, Marriages, 1709-1940:
https://familysearch.org/search/collection/1681011

Pennsylvania, Philadelphia City Births, 1860-1906 :
https://familysearch.org/search/collection/1951739

Pennsylvania, Philadelphia City Death Certificates, 1803-1915:
https://familysearch.org/search/collection/1320976

Pennsylvania, Philadelphia Marriage Indexes, 1885-1951:
https://familysearch.org/search/collection/1388247

Pennsylvania, Pittsburgh City Deaths, 1870-1905:
https://familysearch.org/search/collection/1810412

Census Reports

Census records are among the most important genealogical documents for placing your ancestor in a particular place at a specific time. Like BDM records, they can also lead you to other ancestors, particularly those who were living under the authority of the head of household.

Federal census records for Pennsylvania exist from 1790 –1930 and can be found at:

Pennsylvania State Archives – Federal census records 1790 to 1930, Septennial Census Returns, 1779-1863, United States Direct Tax of 1798: Tax Lists for the State of Pennsylvania

Mailing Address:

350 North Street
Harrisburg, PA 17108-1026
Phone: (717) 783-3281
E-mail: ra-statearchives@state.pa.us

Pennsylvania State Archives:
http://www.portal.state.pa.us/portal/server.pt/community/gene
alogy/3183/census_records/385521

National Archives-Mid-Atlantic Region – Pennsylvania federal census records 1790 - 1930

900 Market Street
Philadelphia, PA 19107-4292
Phone: (215) 606-0100
Fax: (215) 606-0116

National Archives-Mid-Atlantic Region:
http://www.archives.gov/philadelphia/

The **Free Census Project** has transcribed many Pennsylvania indexes and new material is added daily

Free Census Project: http://usgwcensus.org/cenfiles/pa.htm

Access Genealogy – Pennsylvania county census records dating from Colonial times to1930

Access Genealogy:
http://www.accessgenealogy.com/census/pennsylvania-census-records.htm

African American Census Schedules Online – slave schedules, mortality schedules, slave-owners census

African American Census Schedules Online:
http://www.afrigeneas.com/aacensus/ga/

Native Americans in Census Records (US National Archives)

Native Americans in Census Records:
http://www.archives.gov/research/census/native-americans/

<u>Pennsylvania Church Records</u>
Church and synagogue records are a valuable resource, especially for baptisms, marriages, and burials that took place before 1900. You will need to at least have an idea of your ancestor's religious denomination, and in most cases you will have to visit a brick and mortar establishment to view them.

Most church records are kept by the individual church, although in some denominations, records are placed in a regional archive or maintained at the diocesan level. Local Historical Societies are sometimes the repository for the state's older church records. Below are links archives that maintain church records, as well as a few databases that can be viewed online.

The **Family History Library** contains many church records from a variety of denominations on microfilm.

Family History Library:
http://familysearch.org/learn/wiki/en/Family_History_Library

Historical Society of Pennsylvania – large collection of county church records and indexes

1300 Locust Street
Philadelphia, PA 19107
Tel: (215) 732-6200
Fax: (215) 732-2680

Historical Society of Pennsylvania:
http://hsp.org/collections/catalogs-research-tools/subject-guides/family-history-genealogy

Genealogical Society of Pennsylvania – wide variety of county church record indexes and transcriptions and burial and cemetery records histories

2207 Chestnut Street
Philadelphia, PA 19103-3010
Tel: (215) 545-0391

Genealogical Society of Pennsylvania : http://genpa.org/

Central Repositories for Denominational Records

Church of Jesus Christ of Latter-day Saints (Mormons)

Early Mormon Church records for Pennsylvania can be found on film located at the LDS Family History Library in Salt Lake City and can be searched via the **Family History Library Catalog**

Family History Library Catalog:
https://familysearch.org/eng/Library/FHLC/frameset_fhlc.asp

Baptist

American Baptist Historical Society
3001 Mercer University Dr
Atlanta, GA 30341
Telephone: (678) 547-6680

American Baptist Historical Society : http://abhsarchives.org/

Episcopal

Diocese of Pennsylvania
The History Committee
240 S. 4th Street
Philadelphia, PA 19106
Telephone: (215) 627-6434
Fax: (215) 627-7550

Diocese of Pennsylvania : http://www.diopa.org/

Lutheran

Lutheran Archives Center at Philadelphia
Seminary Ridge
Gettysburg PA 17325
Phone: (717) 334-6286, ext 2131

Lutheran Archives Center at Philadelphia:
http://ltsp.edu/lutheran-archives-philadelphia

Tri-Synod Archives at Thiel College
Thiel College
75 College Avenue
Greenville PA 16125
Phone: (724) 589-2131

Tri-Synod Archives at Thiel College:
http://www.thiel.edu/library/Archives1.htm#trisynod

Society of Friends (Quakers)

George Fox College
Quaker Collection
414 N. Meridian Street
Newberg, OR 97132-2697
Phone: (503) 538-8383

George Fox College: http://www.georgefox.edu/

Mennonite

The Mennonite Heritage Center
565 Yoder Road
Harleysville PA 19438-1020
Tel: 215-256-3020
Email: library@mhep.org

The Mennonite Heritage Center : http://mhep.org/

Moravian

The Moravian Archives
41 West Locust Street
Bethlehem, Pennsylvania 18018
United States of America
Phone: (610) 866 3255
Fax: (610) 866-9210

The Moravian Archives :
http://www.moravianchurcharchives.org/general.php

<u>Reformed</u>

Archives of the Evangelical and Reformed Church
Philip Schaff Library
Evangelical and Reformed Historical Library
555 W. James Street
Lancaster, PA 17603
Telephone: (717) 290-8734

Archives of the Evangelical and Reformed Church:
https://www.rca.org/page.aspx?pid=1855

<u>Roman Catholic</u>

Diocese of Allentown
P.O. Box F
Allentown, PA 18105-1538

Diocese of Allentown : http://www.allentowndiocese.org/

Diocese of Altoona
927 S. Logan Boulevard
Hollidaysburg, PA 16648
Phone: (814) 695-5579

Diocese of Altoona: http://www.ajdiocese.org/

Diocese of Erie
St. Mark Catholic Center
429 East Grandview Blvd.
Erie, PA 16504

Diocese of Erie: http://www.eriercd.org/

Diocese of Greensburg
723 East Pittsburgh St.
Greensburg, PA 15601
Phone: (724) 837-0901

Diocese of Greensburg :
http://www.dioceseofgreensburg.org/Pages/default.aspx

Diocese of Harrisburg
4800 Union Deposit Road
Harrisburg, PA 17111
Phone: (717) 657-4804

Diocese of Harrisburg : http://www.hbgdiocese.org/

Archdiocese of Philadelphia
222 North 17th Street,
Philadelphia, PA 19103-1299
Phone: (215) 587-3600

Archdiocese of Philadelphia : http://archphila.org/home.php

Philadelphia Archdiocesan Historical Research Center
100 E. Wynnewood
Wynnewood, PA 19096
Telephone: (610) 667-3394

Philadelphia Archdiocesan Historical Research Center :
http://www.pahrc.net/

Diocese of Pittsburgh
111 Blvd. of the Allies
Pittsburgh, PA 15222
Phone: (412) 456-3000

Diocese of Pittsburgh: http://www.diopitt.org/

Pennsylvania Military Records

More than 40 million Americans have participated in some time of war service since America was colonized. The chance of finding your ancestor amongst those records is exceptionally high. Military records can even reveal individuals who never actually served, such as those who registered for the two World Wars but were never called to duty.

Below are a number of links to websites and archives that contain Pennsylvania military records.

Pennsylvania State Archives – Records for French and Indian War, 1754-1763, Revolutionary War, 1775-1783, The War of 1812,1812-1815, The Mexican War, 1846-1848, Civil War, 1861-1865, Pennsylvania National Guard, 1867-1940, Spanish-American War, 1898-1913, Mexican Border Campaign, 1916-1919
World War I, 1917-1918, World War II, 1941-1945: Bonus Applications, Korean Conflict, 1950-53, Vietnam Conflict, 1961-1975

Mailing Address:

350 North Street
Harrisburg, PA 17108-1026
Phone: (717) 783-3281
E-mail: ra-statearchives@state.pa.us

Pennsylvania State Archives :
http://www.portal.state.pa.us/portal/server.pt?open=512&mode=2&objID=2887

National Archives-Mid-Atlantic Region - Revolutionary War soldiers and pension and bounty land warrants, World War I Draft Registration Cards, original records of the World War II Fourth Enumeration Draft Registration Cards for men from April 1877 to February 1897

900 Market Street
Philadelphia, PA 19107-4292
Phone: (215) 606-0100
Fax: (215) 606-0116

National Archives-Mid-Atlantic Region:
http://www.archives.gov/philadelphia/

US Department of Veterans Affairs Nationwide Gravesite Locator – includes information on veterans and their family members buried in veterans and military cemeteries having a government grave marker.

US Department of Veterans Affairs Nationwide Gravesite Locator: http://gravelocator.cem.va.gov/

You may also find your ancestor's military records in the following databases:

United States General Index to Pension Files, 1861-1934

United States General Index to Pension Files, 1861-1934 : https://familysearch.org/search/collection/1919699

United States Index to Service Records, War with Spain, 1898

United States Index to Service Records, War with Spain, 1898: https://familysearch.org/search/collection/1919583

United States Index to Indian Wars Pension Files, 1892-1926 –
military pension records of soldiers who fought in the Indian Wars
between 1817 and 1898

United States Index to Indian Wars Pension Files, 1892-1926 link
to: https://familysearch.org/search/collection/1979427

United States Registers of Enlistments in the U.S. Army, 1798-1914
- index of men who enlisted in the United States Army, 1798-1914.

United States Registers of Enlistments in the U.S. Army, 1798-1914: https://familysearch.org/search/collection/1880762

United States Mexican War Pension Index, 1887-1926 - index to
Mexican War pension files for service between 1846 and 1848

United States Mexican War Pension Index, 1887-1926 :
https://familysearch.org/search/collection/1979390

Civil War Soldiers Service Records - Service records for both
Union and Confederate soldiers indexed by soldier's name, rank,
and unit.

Civil War Soldier Service Records:
http://go.fold3.com/civilwar_records/

Pennsylvania Cemetery Records

As convenient as it is to search cemetery records online, keep in mind that there are a few disadvantages over visiting a cemetery in person. They are:

- Tombstone information is not always accurately transcribed
- The arrangement of the graves in a cemetery can be crucial as family members are often buried next to each other or in the same grave. This arrangement is not always preserved in the alphabetical indexes that are found online.

With that information in mind, the following websites have databases that can be searched online for Pennsylvania Cemetery records.

Pennsylvania State Library - wide variety of tombstone transcriptions from a variety of Pennsylvania townships and boroughs

607 South Drive
Harrisburg, Pennsylvania
Phone: (717) 783-5950

Pennsylvania State Library :
http://www.portal.state.pa.us/portal/server.pt/community/ceme taries___obituaries/8731/zeamer_collection__cumberland_county

Pennsylvania Tombstone Transcription Project - death and burial records

Pennsylvania Tombstone Transcription Project:
http://www.usgwtombstones.org/pennsylvania/pennsyl.html

African American Cemeteries Online – African American, slave, and Native American cemetery records
African American Cemeteries Online:
http://africanamericancemeteries.com/ar/

Access Genealogy – database of Pennsylvania cemetery record transcriptions
Access Genealogy:
http://www.accessgenealogy.com/cemetery/pennsylvania-cemetery-records.htm

Find a Grave – over 100 million grave records can be searched on this site. Search can be conducted by name, location, or cemetery name.
Find a Grave: http://www.findagrave.com/

Interment.net - A free online database containing approximately 4 million cemetery records from around the world.
Interment.net link to: http://www.interment.net/

Billion Graves – as the name implies, you can search a billion records including headstone photos, transcriptions, cemetery records, and grave locations.
Billion Graves:
http://billiongraves.com/pages/search/index.php#cemetery

Pennsylvanian Obituaries

Obituaries can reveal a wealth about our ancestor and other relatives. You can search our **Pennsylvania Obituaries Listings** from hundreds of Pennsylvania newspapers online for free.

Pennsylvania Obituaries Listings:
http://obituarieshelp.org/pennsylvania_newspaper_obituaries.html

Pennsylvania Wills and Probate Records

The documents found in a probate packet may include a complete inventory of a person's estate, newspaper entries, witness testimony, a copy of a will, list of debtors and creditors, names of executors or trustees, names of heirs. They can not only tell you about the ancestor you're currently researching, but lead to other ancestors.

Probate records in Pennsylvania were kept in **Pennsylvania County Courts** since the origin of the Commonwealth in 1682, and complete records are available in most counties.

Pennsylvania County Courts :
http://www.pacourts.us/courts/courts-of-common-pleas/district-court-administrators

You may also find Pennsylvania Probate records at:

Historical Society of Pennsylvania - Abstracts of Philadelphia Wills: 1682-1825, Index To Philadelphia Wills & Administrations: 1682-1850, Philadelphia Wills: 1682-1900.

1300 Locust Street
Philadelphia, PA 19107
Tel: (215) 732-6200
Fax: (215) 732-2680

Historical Society of Pennsylvania :
http://hsp.org/collections/catalogs-research-tools/subject-guides/family-history-genealogy

Pennsylvania State Archives – variety of county wills, estate inventories, and deeds

Mailing Address:

350 North Street
Harrisburg, PA 17108-1026
Phone: (717) 783-3281
E-mail: ra-statearchives@state.pa.us

Pennsylvania State Archives:
http://www.portal.state.pa.us/portal/server.pt/community/land_records/3184/county_and_municipal_records/439671

Family Search has the following online index which can be searched for free:

1. **Pennsylvania, Probate Records, 1683-1994**

Pennsylvania, Probate Records, 1683-1994:
https://familysearch.org/search/collection/1999196

Pennsylvania Immigration and Naturalization Records

The naturalization process generated many types of records, including petitions, declarations of intention, and oaths of allegiance. These records can provide family historians with information such as a person's birth date and place of birth, immigration year, marital status, spouse information, occupation, witnesses' names and addresses, and more.

Pennsylvania State Archives – Naturalization lists of the Supreme Court and Courts of Nisi Prius for the years 1740-1773; Naturalization records of the Supreme Court of Pennsylvania, 1794-1868; county naturalization records, ships' passenger lists recording the arrival of Continental Europeans (chiefly German, Dutch, Swiss and French) at the Port of Philadelphia, 1727-1744, 1746-1756, 1761, 1763-1775, 1785-1808.

Mailing Address:

350 North Street
Harrisburg, PA 17108-1026
Phone: (717) 783-3281
E-mail: ra-statearchives@state.pa.us

Pennsylvania State Archives:
http://www.portal.state.pa.us/portal/server.pt?open=512&mode=2&objID=2887

Genealogical Society of Pennsylvania - Philadelphia Courts Naturalization Index, 1790 - 1880

2207 Chestnut Street
Philadelphia, PA 19103-3010
Tel: (215) 545-0391

Genealogical Society of Pennsylvania : http://genpa.org/

National Archives-Mid-Atlantic Region – Philadelphia, Indexes 1800-1948, Passenger Lists 1800-1945, Atlantic and Gulf Ports (small ports) Index 1820-1874, Passenger Lists 1820-1873, Naturalizations Philadelphia, 1790-1991; Pittsburgh, 1820-1979; Erie, 1940-1972; Scranton, 1901-1990; Wilkes-Barre, 1943-1972; Williamsport, 1909-1913; and Harrisburg, 1911-1917

900 Market Street
Philadelphia, PA 19107-4292
Phone: (215) 606-0100
Fax: (215) 606-0116

National Archives-Mid-Atlantic Region:
http://www.archives.gov/philadelphia/

Family Search has the following online indexes which can be searched for free:

Pennsylvania, Eastern District Naturalization Indexes, 1795-1952 :
https://familysearch.org/search/collection/1937344

Pennsylvania, Eastern District Petitions for Naturalization, 1795-1931: https://familysearch.org/search/collection/1913395

Pennsylvania, Philadelphia Case Files of Chinese Immigrants, 1900-1923: https://familysearch.org/search/collection/1888682

Pennsylvania, Philadelphia Passenger List Index Cards, 1883-1948 : https://familysearch.org/search/collection/1921483

Pennsylvania, Philadelphia Passenger Lists, 1800-1882: https://familysearch.org/search/collection/1908535

Pennsylvania, Philadelphia Passenger Lists, 1883-1945: https://familysearch.org/search/collection/1921481

Pennsylvania Native American Records
Historical Society of Pennsylvania - Indian Rights Association records, 1830-1986.

1300 Locust Street
Philadelphia, PA 19107
Tel: (215) 732-6200
Fax: (215) 732-2680

Historical Society of Pennsylvania:
http://hsp.org/collections/catalogs-research-tools/subject-guides/family-history-genealogy

Access Genealogy – Pennsylvania Native American census records, tribal histories, and much more

Access Genealogy :
http://www.accessgenealogy.com/native/pennsylvania-indian-tribes.htm

U.S. National Archives - information on American Indians who maintained their ties to Federally-recognized Tribes (1830-1970).

U.S. National Archives:
http://www.archives.gov/research/native-americans/

Records of the Bureau of Indian Affairs (BIA)

Records of the Bureau of Indian Affairs (BIA):
http://www.archives.gov/research/guide-fed-records/groups/075.html

American Indians Records Repository - records dating from the 1700s including trust, education and other historic Indian Affairs records

American Indian Records Repository
Meritex Enterprises
17501 West 98th Street
Lenexa, KS 66219
Phone: 913-888-0601

American Indians Records Repository:
http://www.doi.gov/ost/records_mgmt/american-indian-records-repository.cfm

Missing Matriarchs – Resources for Researching Female Pennsylvania Ancestors

Looking for female ancestors requires an adjustment of how we view traditional records sources. A woman's identity was often under that of her husband, and often individual records for them can be difficult to locate. The following resources are effective in locating female ancestors in Pennsylvania where traditional records may not reveal them.

<u>Bibliographies</u>

- *Keeping House: Women's Lives in Western Pennsylvania, 1790-1850,* Virginia K. Bartlett (Historical Society of Western Pennsylvania and University of Pittsburgh Press, 1994)
- *Women of the Trades: Pittsburgh, 1907-1908,* Elisabeth Butler (University of Pittsburgh Press, 1984)
- *The Homespun Textile Tradition of the Pennsylvania Germans,* Ellen Gehret and Alan G. Keyser (Pennsylvania Historic Commission, 1976)
- *Women and Quakerism,* Hope E. Luder (Pendle Hill, 1974)
- *Runaway Women: Elopements and Other Miscreant Deeds of Women, As Advertised in the Pennsylvania Gazette,* Judith Ann Meyer (Closson Press, 1993)
- *Mennonite Women: A Sturdy of God's Faithfulness, 1683-1983,* E.S.Rich (Kitchner Herald, 1983)

Selected Resources for Pennsylvania Women's History

American Quilt Museum
Market and New Haven Streets
Marietta, PA 17547-0065

Philadelphia College of Textiles and Science
Pastore Library
School House Lane and Henry Avenue
Philadelphia, PA 19144

Women's Studies Collection
Cressman Library
Cedar Crest College
Cedar Crest Boulevard
Allentown, PA 18104

Common Pennsylvania Surnames

The following surnames are among the most common in Pennsylvania and are also being currently researched by other genealogists. If you find your surname here, there is a chance that some research has already been performed on your ancestor.

ABRAHAMSON, ADAMO, ADAMS, ALEXANDER, ALVORD, AMUNDSON, ANDREWS, ARNOLD, ASH, BACKSTROM, BAISE, BALL, BANKS, BARBUTO, BARNARD, BARNEY, BECELLA, BEGER, BEGGARLY, BELEHER, BELINI, BELLOWS, BELT, BERGMAN, BERKINS, BIELAWSKI, BILLBROUGH, BISHOP, BISSETT, BLANCHARD, BLEVINS, BLIKSTAD, BODE, BOEHM, BOMAN, BORLAND, BOYD, BRADEN, BRADY, BRITTON, BROGAN, BROUCKE, BROWN, BRUNI, BRUSVEN, BRYANT, BUCHANAN, BUCHOLTZ, BUCZEK, BUNGE, BURMEISTER, CALDWELL, CAMERON, CANNON, CARCABA, CAREY, CARLSON, CARMICHAEL, CASE, CELINSKI, CHAMBERS, CHAPMAN, CHRISTOPHERSON, CHROBAK, CICHY, CLARK, CLASEN, COASTER, COLBURN, COLLINS, COLVIN, COLWELL, CONNELL, COOKMAN, COULSON, COULTON, CRAGE, CRAWFORD, CRISCI, CUTTER, DABROSKI, DABROWSKI, DANIELS, DANIELSON, DASSOW, DAVIDSON, DAVIS, DAYTON, DE NATO, DEAN, DEICH, DEMBICKI, DEPA, DERDA, DIMOCK, DOAK, DODDY, DOEHRING, DOLATA, DOLBEER, DOMBROWSKI, DOMHOLT, DORSEY, DOSTIE, DOUGLAS, DUGAN, DUNLAP, DWORNICZAK, EALY, EASPELERN, EAVENSON, EDWARDS, EHFARTH, ELIASON, ELLIOT, ELLISON, ENGH, ENGLISH, ENSLIN, ESCH, EVERS, EYLER, FARABEE, FEIST, FERALDO, FERROL, FIYZGERALD, FLETCHER, FOGLEY, FOUCHER, FRANTZ, FRESHWATER, FRY, FULLER, FURBEE, GALANTOWCZ, GARBERG, GARCIA, GARDNER, GARDULSKI, GARY, GIBSON, GIGERICH, GILLESPIE, GLOVER, GODFREY, GOETTEL, GORSLINE, GRABOWSKI, GRAHAM, GREEN, GREENE, GREENUP, GRIFKA, HALCIK, HALL, HANSON, HARPER, HATALA, HAZELETT, HEDWIG, HEEBNER, HEINCER, HEROUX, HEWITT, HICKS, HOLMES, HOOP, HOPPER, HORNER, HOWE, HUFFMAN, HUMPHREY, HUNT, HUOVINEN, IRWIN, IVISON, JACKSON, JACOBS, JAMES, JANKOWSKA, JANKOWSKI, JAWAAD, JEFFERY, JOHNSON, JOHNSTON, JONES, JUNTUNEN, KELLER, KELLY, KEMPPAINEN, KENWORTHY, KERLIN, KETCHUM, KETLAR, KETLER, KETTLAR, KETTLER, KING, KINSMAN, KLECZYNSKI, KNOPF, KNUTSON, KOCHANOWSKA, KOCHANOWSKI, KONICKA, KONICKI, KOSEK, KRAMER,

KREMMER, KROTKIEWCZ, KRUIZE, KRYZOSTAN, KUBE, KUBE-MCDOWELL, KUNKEL, KYLE, KYNER, LAMBRECHT, LANDWEHR, LARSON, LAUGEN, LAW, LAWRENCE, LAZANO, LEACH, LEEPER, LEIN, LESINSKI, LEWANDOWSKI, LINDQUIST, LISIECKI, LITTLE, LLOYD, LOCKERT, LOMBARDO, LONG, LUDWIG, LUKASCZAWSKI, MADDEN, MADEJA, MALCOMB, MALINCZAK, MALLOY, MARENDA, MARKLEY, MARPLE, MARSTON, MATTHEWS, MAUER, MAYER, MAYKA, MCBRIDE, MCCALL, MCCANN, MCCLURE, MCCONAGHEY, MCCOWEN, MCCOY, MCCRACKEN, MCDOWEL, MCDOWELL, MCGILL, MCKENZIE, MCKEON, MCKIBBEN, MCKINNEY, MCMACHEN, MCMULLEN, MCNAMARA, MCQUEEN, MCQUILLIAM, MEDBURY, MEINHARDT, MELDRIM, MERCER, MEREDITH, MEYERS, MICHCZYNSKI, MIGLEO, MIJARES, MILDE, MILFORD, MILLER, MITCHELL, MOLLOY, MONKIEWICZ, MOORE, MOSLEY, MUNGER, MURREY, MUSSELMAN, MUTSCH, MYCZEK, MYERS, NASH, NEULIEB, NEUMARK, NICHCZYNSKI, NORRIS, NORWOOD, NOWADROWSKI, NOWAK, NOWODWORSKI, NUGENT, OLDS, O'NEILL, PACKARD, PARGMAN, PARKINSON, PARKS, PARYASKI, PECK, PEDRICK, PERRI, PETERS, PETERSON, PETIT, PHILLIPS, PHIPPS, PIERCE, PILZNER, PILZNINSKI, PIPER, PLANTS, PORTER, POSTULA, PRASKEY, PRICE, PROVCHY, R., RADNIECKI, RAHOCZY, REESER, REGIEC, REINHOLD, RIDDLE, RIHA, ROBBINS, ROBERTS, RODDY, ROGERS, ROSS, ROSSMAN, ROSSOW, ROVICH, RUSH, RUSSELL, RYBICKA, SANDECKI, SASTOW, SAVAGE, SAVILLE, SCARLES, SCHAEFFER, SCHOEN, SCHULTZ, SCOTT, SCZMANSKI, SHELBERG, SHUNKO, SIMMONS, SIMON, SIMPSON, SKELDON, SKERRATT, SKYSTAD, SLAWEK, SLOAN, SMAGA, SMITH, SPANGLER, SQUIRE, STANLEY, STARIN, STAWICK, STAWICKI, STEELE, STEVENS, STEWART, STOKES, STOLLAR, STORTROEN, SURITH, SYMS, SZCZENIOWSKI, TAYLOR, THOMAS, THOMPSON, THORSEN, THORSON, TOPE, TOWNSEND, TREPPA, TROELSEH, TROMPOINSKA, TURENE, TUSTIN, USKO, VALENTINE, VANNOY, VASKO, VAUSCOY, VESEY, VOSSEN, VUKMIROVICH, WALDORF, WALLS, WAMER, WARD, WARDWELL, WATSON, WAY, WEBB, WEIDENBACH, WEIDNER, WELCH, WELLEN, WELSAND, WENTZEL, WHITAKER, WILLSON, WITULSKI, WOLK, WONSIK, WRAY, WRIJEL, WYTOLA, ZAK, ZAKRZEWSKI